The Footprints

of

God

Recognizing God's
Presence in the Ordinary

Sister Kathleen M. O'Connell, RSM

THE BEAUTY OF CREATION BEARS WITNESS TO GOD
by St. Augustine (Public Domain)

Question the beauty of the earth,
the beauty of the sea,
the beauty of the wide air around you,
the beauty of the sky;
question the order of the stars,
the sun whose brightness lights the days,
the moon whose splendor softens the gloom of night;
question the living creatures that move in the waters,
that roam upon the earth,
that fly through the air;
the spirit that lies hidden,
the matter that is manifest;
the visible things that are ruled,
the invisible things that rule them;
question all these.

They will answer you: "Behold and see, we are beautiful."
Their beauty is their confession to God.

Who made these beautiful changing things,
if not one who is beautiful and changeth not?

Introduction

This book began as a response to a challenge. In the spring of 2018, the leadership of the Sisters of Mercy of the Americas offered a challenge to its members and associates. On December 21, 2018, the Sisters of Mercy would be celebrating the 175th Anniversary of their first arrival in the United States to the city of Pittsburgh. To give special meaning to this event, we were challenged to do 175 works of Mercy. Throughout the United States, the sisters, their associates, their students and friends accepted the challenge and soon there were 175 lunches prepared for the homeless, 175 pairs of winter socks collected, 175 hand knitted scarves, 175 notes written to shut-ins, 175 Rosaries prayed, and countless more acts of mercy.

Using my gift of photography, I decided to send, via the internet, a nature photograph each day for 175 days leading up to the celebration in December. Each photo would be accompanied by a scripture verse and short reflection. And I would send it to at least 175 people.

This endeavor would also include one of the critical concerns of the Sisters of Mercy, that of our care for the earth, for its sustainability and vitality. The daily photograph and reflection reminds us that we have been gifted with this earth by our Creator and that we are called, each one of us, to be faithful stewards of that which has been entrusted to us. Our stewardship takes place not in enormous expenditures of time and money but in the countless little things we do each day to better our environment and protect it for future generations.

This book is not intended to be read cover to cover in one reading. Instead, it offers the possibility to take a brief moment in time to recall the wonders our God has done for us. Each reflection is how the Spirit spoke to me. The Spirit may speak to you with different words. My prayer is that the photos will guide you to a deeper recognition of the Presence of God in his created world, and that this will lead to a deeper commitment to your stewardship of his creation.

In Appreciation

I am grateful for the many words of encouragement and appreciation for the daily photos and reflections. It has been overwhelming. Thank you to the many who sent messages and sent "Likes" on Facebook.

I have been blessed to have many who have encouraged this book:

First, gratitude to our God: Creator, Savior, Spirit. It has been an awesome experience to sit in front of a blank computer screen and find the words begin to flow. Only the Spirit could give this miracle.

The gift of being able to "see" with the lens of a camera has been a great joy. To be able to use this gift to enable others to "see" the wonders of God's creation and to encourage them to care for it, has been an honor.

I am grateful for those who have walked with me in the processing of this book: my Sisters in Mercy, associates, friends, and family whose encouragement have kept me on track. I am grateful to Patty Cost who has guided me through the intricacies of Adobe InDesign computer program that is used for this book. I am grateful for her expertize, suggestions and advice. Thank you, Patty. Thank you to my "once an English teacher, always an English teacher" friend, Sister Marlene Vigna, who proofed my typed manuscript. If we missed any mistakes, it is all my fault. It is with a thankful heart that I acknowledge Mary Kerr and Tom O'Connell, whose generous gifts helped to enable the printing of this book. Thank you, Mary and Tom.

Lastly, and certainly not least, I am grateful to my parents, Isabelle and Flerence O'Connell, who first introduced me to God's creation. Their flower and vegetable gardens awakened in me an awareness that all of creation is a Gift of God; their care for the earth showed me how to appreciate this gift. I dedicate this book in their memory.

Tell
God's glory
among the nations;
among all peoples
God's marvelous
deeds.

Ps 96:3

A walk along the Sea Breeze pier is what is needed at the end of the day. Breezes blowing off the water cool the air from the day's heat. The sun sets to mark the closure of the day's activities. How did you spend this day? Did you run out of time to do all you had planned? Did surprises come your way in unexpected encounters? Ending each day with some reflective moments prepares us for the tomorrow that is yet to come. Who were the people in this day? What is yet to be finished tomorrow? Did you look at the interruptions in your plans as time wasted or as opportunities to listen, reach out, perhaps offer a helping hand? I have yet to meet a person whose day went exactly as planned. That's what makes the coming of a new day exciting. What surprises has God prepared for you tomorrow? The setting sun gives us the promise of a new day. What is left of today is yours to relax and enjoy. Tomorrow has its own possibilities.

*Great
are the works
of the Lord,
to be
treasured
for all their
delights.*

Ps. 111:2

Maplewood Rose Garden is an oasis of beauty on the finge of the city, and is noted for its amazing display of roses: all colors, varieties, scents. Its June Rose Festival brings many visitors to see the roses in their first bloom. This is one of them. It is a quiet place in spite of its nearness to a main traffic thoroughfare. You can park yourself at a picnic table to eat your lunch and observe the bountiful variety of roses. There is a feeling of reverence as people quietly stroll through the grassy lawn, a prayerfulness as they bend down to smell the fragrances. How wonderful it is to have places like this where we can get in touch with nature if only for a little while. With gratitude we acknowledge the gift of the place, and thank all those who continue to make it a haven of beauty in the midst of a busy city.

Maplewood Rose Garden, Lake Ave., Rochester, NY

Twice a day, guided by the tidal pull of the moon, waves crash upon the Atlantic shore. The surf leaps to jump over the rocky barrier and splashes with great force. The moment can be captured by a quick click of the camera and then it is gone. Endlessly pounding the shore with a force strong enough to move even these boulders, the rhythm of the ocean continues day after day. In between the moments of incoming tide, are the moments when the water gently laps the shoreline, slowly ebbing and flowing. And so it is with God's great love for each of us. God's love is everlasting, sometimes gentle, sometimes forceful. Constant is the Lord's love. The ocean reminds me of that.

Crashing Surf, Hampton Beach, NH

Notice how
the flowers grow...
they do not toil nor spin.
But I tell you, not even
Solomon in all his
splendor was dressed
like one of them.
If God so clothes the
grass of the field that
grows today and tomor-
row is tossed into the
fire, will he not provide
much more for you?

Luke 12:27

Startled by a sudden spray from the rotating sprinkler, I quickly turned away from the water source and found myself looking behind me at a diamond studded peony. The water droplets sparkled in the sun and gave an exquisite appearance to what was already a lovely flower. And I almost missed it. Too engrossed in what lay ahead, I neglected to see where I had already been. God's gentle splash of a sprinkler caused me to look back. How often do we do this, look to the future, whether it be the next fifteen minutes, or next week or month but neglect what have been jewel encrusted moments of the present. Too quickly we forget how we have been blessed by the Lord because we are too occupied with forging ahead to the next thing. Sometimes we need a gentle shove to remind us that blessedness often comes in little moments, the little droplets of beauty that come along our path. Thank you, Lord, for the sudden surprise of a sprinkler.

Secret Walk, Beach Ave. Rochester, NY

"What do you want me to do for you?" The blind man replied to him, "Master, I want to see."

Mark 10:51

This rice-paper butterfly posed for me at Butterfly World in Niagara Falls. It seems that every butterfly photo I have taken shows the butterfly perched on a cheerful, bright-colored flower. Attracted by the colors, it seeks the inner goodness of the flower, the positive side of the flower whether it be a weed or an exotic bloom. What do you seek? The bright colors of the positive or the grays of the negative? What's in your garden?

*You made
the moon to mark
the seasons;
The sun knows the
hour of its setting.
Lord,
How varied are
your works, Lord!
In wisdom you have
wrought them all.*

Ps. 104:19,

Full moon tonight. Oh my goodness! It's caught! Will it be freed by dawn? Of course! The moon knows its place in the universe. It is faithful to its Creator!
Are we?

Moon Rise. Madison, CT

*After this
I had a vision
of a great
multitude, which
no one could
count, from ev-
ery nation, race,
people and
tongue.*

Rev. 7:9

This rocky road in Northern Ireland is not one you would choose if you were in a hurry to get somewhere. It is a road that must be driven with care and full attention. In spite of its difficulty, it is a road that is traveled. People have journeyed this way and their tracks are like a guide taking you safely to the top of the hill and beyond. Life can sometimes be like this road, a bit uncertain and bumpy for a stretch and then smooth and easier other times. We are not alone on this Way. Others have gone before us and have shown us how to navigate the rougher times and how to enjoy the smoother ones. Some names we recognize: Peter, Augustine, Francis, Theresa of Calcutta, Oscar, John Paul. Others we know as Mom, Dad, Grandma, Grandpa, teacher, nurse, firefighter, friend. We follow their tracks as they teach us patience, compassion, mercy, kindness, love. What tracks will we leave for those coming behind?

Daylilies have their blooming time usually from late June to August. Once they are established in a garden, or even on the side of the road, they multiply rapidly. Because of hybridization, the daylily now comes in a variety of colors as is this red one in the photo. No longer just the orange variety, there are yellows, pinks, red, even blue daylilies. Consider the possibilities of a garden filled with so many different color varieties. Normally, the day lily is just that – a bloom that lasts only a day. We don't recognize that often because the plant offers so many buds during its blooming season. Life is like that somewhat. People of different varieties come into our lives and stay but a short while but we are left with the beauty of the meeting and the fragrance of their presence. Our garden is forever changed because of their having traveled through it with us. Who has enhanced your garden?

There shall always be rejoicing and happiness in what I create.

Isaiah 65:18

Summer Lily, Rochester, NY

...Hide me in the shadow of your wings.

Ps. 17:8

Mama swan was sitting on her nest in the pond along the side of the road in Durand Eastman Park. She looked so peaceful there, belying the fact that there was much going on unseen. Suddenly, out from under her wing popped a little head, curious about the world around it. Gradually it was followed by 7 more little heads, all eager to get out and explore. Their first swim – like ducks taking to water. Well, of course! How glorious are the miracles of spring. New life all around us, ours for the looking. Miracles showing us God's love are found in every part of our lives. Each season has its own miracles. We just need to recognize them. Often they are right in front of our eyes but sometimes we have to look under the wings.

The Swan Family, Durand Eastman Park on the shores of
Lake Ontario, Rochester, NY

The southwest of the United States offers some fabulous views as you travel along the edge of Colorado toward Bryce Canyon. Colorado in Spanish means "colored red" and that aptly describes the many rock formations you will see there. We know that these formations didn't happen yesterday. God did not point a finger and say "Be a red rock formation and have a funny shape." No, it happened millions of yesterdays ago as God unleashed the forces of nature, shaping the earth. These rock formations are not yet complete. They will continue to change through millions of tomorrows. So too, we are not yet complete. We continue to grow and develop through the days of our lives. Each of us has the potential for great things in God's kingdom. They may not be realized today, or even tomorrow. Perhaps understanding that will help us to overlook the shortcomings of others. Still, all the works of the Lord are glorious. We are the masterpieces of God's creation. We are people of great promise. What do you see as your promise?

Majestic and glorious your work, your wise design endures for ever.

Ps. 111:3

Red Stone Rocks and Hoodoos in south western Utah

*Find your
delight in the
Lord
who will give
you your
heart's
desire.*

Ps 37:4

It was a busy little monarch that was leading me on a merry chase in a garden in Salem, MA. But it settled long enough for a "Kodak" moment. Sometimes our lives can cause us to feel as if we are butterflies, flitting from one thing to another. "Busyness" seems to be our middle name as we consult our check list of "To Do's." Cross one task off and add another. No wonder we feel worn out at the end of the day. It helps if we are able to take a little break every so often. Maybe not everything on the list needs to be done today. Even butterflies need to stop for a moment.

Monarch flitting about in a private garden in Salem, MA

Be still and know that I am God.   Ps. 46:10

Energy pulsates out from this water lily basking in the sun at McKee Gardens, Vero Beach, FL. It speaks to me of the mercy of God that radiates out from a heart centered in God. To be so centered one has to simply listen to God speaking within. The Mercy of God has a radiance all its own.

Water Lily at McKee Gardens, Vero Beach, FL

The attendants at African Safari at Seneca Park Zoo (Rochester) had just finished giving Lilac (or is it Jenny) a bath in the barn. She promptly went out and found the water hole, and began to cover herself with the mud. So much for all their hard work. "A chocolate-covered elephant!" I laughed. Perfect for a hot summer day. Laughter, they say, is good for the soul. When was your last big belly laugh? The definition of humor says it is a comic, absurd, or incongruous quality causing amusement. Look for something today that tickles your funny bone. And laugh!

Sarah then said, "God has given me cause to laugh, and all who hear of it will laugh with me."

Genesis 21:6

Resident of the African Exhibit at Seneca Park Zoo, Rochester, NY

Powerscourt Waterfalls in the Wicklow Mts. is the highest waterfall in Ireland. To gauge its height of 398 feet, compare the two people standing next to the bottom of the tree on the left with the height of the falls. A beautiful spot for picnickers! Interestingly, Google cites only one reference to the word "waterfalls" in the New American Bible (used here). Instead, it offers a number of references to God's overflowing love, the power and the steadfastness of God's love, the work of the Spirit in the lives of God's people. In other words, "waterfalls" are a symbol of God's love for us. Never ending, powerful, life-giving, cleansing, present, continuous, ... God's love is everlasting.

Deep calls to deep at the roar of your torrents.
All your waves and breakers have swept over me.
Ps 42:7

May the
Lord
bless
his people
with
peace.

Ps. 29:11

Another flower from the Creator's hands. Who knew there could be so many different kinds of orchids? Can't pronounce, let alone spell, the name of this one. This somehow reminds me of those little holy water fonts we had at the doorways of our rooms. We would dip our fingers in the holy water and bless ourselves with the sign of the cross. It was a reminder that God was with us in our comings and goings. We seem to have lost this tradition. What would our day be like if these little fonts again reminded us that our day has been and is blessed?

Taken at the annal Orchid Show at Eisenhart Theater, Rochester, NY

Thorns and thistles shall it bring forth to you, as you eat of the plants of the field.

Genesis 3:18

The first mention of thistles in scripture occurs right after Adam and Eve are banished from the Garden of Eden. Thistles have been around a long time. The internet lists over a hundred plus kinds of thistles that exist all over the world. Thistles are considered an invasive weed that sports a pretty flower and prickly, sharp thorns or spikes. They won't be first on a list for a floral display. Yet, before dismissing them as simply weeds, look at their beauty and usefulness. They feed the larvae of many different butterflies, esp. the swallowtail butterfly. They provide food for pollinators, and their seeds are used for feeding the little finches. In some countries they are even used for human consumption. See what good can come from even a weed! Praise the Lord for prickly little weeds!

Thistle in the garden of Mercy by the Sea, Madison, CT

The Black River begins at North Lake in the Adirondacks Mts and flows for 125 miles until it empties out into eastern Lake Ontario. Fed by numerous streams and creeks, it can at times be powerful with many rapids. Other times, it meanders peacefully through the Adirondacks valley, bringing a calm and gentle flow. Carey Landry's hymn *"Peace is Flowing Like a River"* comes to mind when I look at this photo and remember this place. The waters move along gently here, bringing that peace I need in my heart. But the operative word here is "flowing." Peace is not ours to keep but a gift from God to be passed on to others. *"Peace,"* indeed, *"is flowing out of you and me"* to nourish the hearts of others. Peace is not stagnant but a living, moving part of the human soul.

For thus says the Lord: "Behold, I will extend prosperity over her like a river, and the wealth of the nations like an overflowing torrent".

Isaiah 66:12

Black River, Adirondacks Mt., Boonville, NY

The Lord said, "Go out and stand on the mountain in the presence of the Lord, for the Lord is about to pass by."

1 Kings 19:11

Mountains are symbols of encounters with God. In the Hebrew and Christian scriptures, mountains are mentioned over 500 times. Not surprising for a land filled with mountains. They are places where important encounters with the Lord have taken place. The quote today describes Elijah's meeting with the Lord on Mt. Horeb. Elijah recognizes that the Lord is not in the earthquakes, nor the fires, but instead in a quiet whispering sound. And Elijah hid his face. Do we need to climb a mountain to find the Lord? Of course not, but we do need the quiet and stillness found on mountain tops. For it is in that quiet and stillness that we can hear the voice of the Lord. These are sacred places, our mountain tops, and we build holy altars in our hearts so as to hear God's quiet, whispering voice. We are invited to come by the Lord himself.

Sierra Nevada Mountains, western Nevada

If I fly with the wings of dawn and alight beyond the sea –
even there your hand will still guide me,
your right hand hold me fast. Ps. 139:9, 10

The majestic soaring of the sea gull, (or any winged creature), reminds me that no matter how high or how far I go, God is always with me. Though I may not realize it at the moment, I know it to be true. God's right hand may be the hand of a friend, a kind word, a beautiful flower, a golden sunset. Where do you feel God's right hand upholding you right now?

Soaring seagull, Hampton Beach, NH

Two butterflies pose for a photo at Butterfly World, Niagara, Canada. Seemingly so carefree as they flit about the leaves, we forget the major transformation that has taken place in their brief lives, the change from larvae to beautiful wings. That chrysalis holds promise for us as we risk the changes that take place in our own lives. Do we have the faith to believe that God is with us in these changes, that he walks the journey along side us? We may not yet know what is to be but we have faith that whatever transformation occurs, it will be something beautiful.

We walk by faith, not by sight. 2 Corinthians 5:7

Butterfly World, Niagara Falls, CA

Blessed
are the eyes
that see what
you see.

Luke 19:41

You never know what you will see when you look at the backside of something. This back view of a hibiscus where it fastens to the stem shows a five-pointed star. The light shining through the petals gives a new appreciation for the details of the flower. Colors are more intense and shadows more mysterious. Both sides of the flower gift us with a glimpse of beauty. Focusing too much on one side causes us to miss the gift of the other side. Isn't that true of life? When we focus too much on one side of a person, thing, or action, we miss the promise of another view – from the other side. We realize that there is more than one way to look at things.

Hindsight, back view of a neighbor's hibiscus

These Irish dancers and musicians illustrate another very creative side of God: that of music and dance. Through the centuries, since the beginning of creation, people have made music and have danced to its melodies. Whether it is knocking two sticks together in rhythm, shaking a box of shells or pebbles, playing a Stradivarius violin or a cathedral organ, music has been the heartbeat of humanity. It calms, soothes, rocks, and ignites the human soul. Dance moves the body to the music of the waltz, the Charleston, the twist, or quiet toe tapping. Listen today to some music. Turn off the TV and find some form of music to listen to. Just sit quietly in its rhythm and let it soak in. Maybe even dance to its sound. Praise your God with music.

These Irish dancers and musicians are at the entrance of a cultural centre in Ireland at the foot of the Rock of Cashal, Co. Tipperary. The Bru Boru Centre celebrates the folk arts of the Irish/Celtic people and is alive with all kinds of music Irish.

My heart is steadfast, God;
I will sing and chant praise.
Awake my soul, awake the lyre and harp.
I will wake the dawn.

Ps. 108:1,2

John Muir (1834-1914) was an early advocate for the preservation of the wilderness in our country and an activist for the creation of the National Park system. He is most particularly connected with Yosemite National Park. These centuries old redwoods just north of San Francisco. are in Muir Woods named for him. In light of the many thousands of acres of California that have been burned in recent months, his words give us hope. *"The redwood is one of the few conifers that sprout from the stump and roots, and it declares itself willing to begin immediately to repair the damage of the lumberman and also that of the forest-burner."* John Muir Reforestation has begun – initiated by the very trees that were burned. New life is within us. Instead of being overwhelmed by the blackened stumps, we need only to look for the signs of new life. Expect to find it.

Then shall the trees of the forest exult before the Lord for he comes to rule the earth.

1 Chronicles 16:33

Ancient redwoods in Muir Woods, CA

*But some
seed fell on
rich soil, and
produced
fruit –
a hundred,
sixty or thirty
fold.*

Mt. 13:8

These fields provide the fresh fruits and vegetables that are sold at Wilson's Farm Market in Lexington, MA. When I was growing up, my Dad had a vegetable farm. In the spring he spent hours tilling the soil, preparing it for the new crop of vegies. Failure to do this would result in a dismal crop. So, while it was hard work, his labors paid off 100, 60, 30 times. Sometimes there were just too many turnips for me! What am I doing to till the soil of my heart to make it "good soil?" What choices do I make that will provide the nourishment needed for me to produce the hundred, sixty or thirty-fold? It is hard work, this work of tilling the spiritual soil. But it is worth it.

God made all kinds of wild animals...
God saw how good it was. Genesis 1:25

Another one of God's fun creations. The meerkat is not a "kat" at all. It is a weasel-like animal that lives in burrows under the ground. Found in the southern portion of Africa, they live in large groups of 10 to 40 called a "mob." This particular meerkat lives at Seneca Park Zoo, Rochester, NY. Meerkat mobs spend a lot of their time grooming and playing together to keep the family as a tight unit. This community existence helps the meerkats survive. They have their own "neighborhood watch," warning of impending attack by predators. Their long claws are necessary both for digging burrows and for gathering food. they give us another reason to rejoice in God's creation, and to reflect on what it means to be "community."

Bridges are utilitarian. They function to enable us to cross over something, to transition from one place to another. In this case, it is to connect the two sides of the river bank. The person walking the bridge may be unaware of the beautiful flowers growing out of the rocky structure. Yet, once the person has crossed and looks back at the bridge from the distance, he sees the inherent beauty of the bridge. We cross many bridges during our lifetime. Some are natural transitions: finishing school, a new job, marriage, deaths. Some are unexpected transitions: poor health, accidents, loss of a job, broken relationships. While in the experience of crossing the bridge, of making a transition, we often are not aware of the beauty of the moment. Nor are we aware of who has been traveling this bridge with us. It is only when we look back at where we have been that we see the flowers blooming, where God has been in this transition. And we rejoice in what God has done for us.

Jesus said to him, (Thomas), "I am the way, and the truth and the life."

John 14:6

Flowering Bridge in Co. Limmerick, Ireland

Consider the lilies. How beautiful they are. Not even Solomon looked so good in all his finery! The color! The detail! The lacy edge of the bloom! Another exquisite creation of the Lord! We would never consider calling it a weed, something useless, for no good purpose. Now go look in the mirror. What do you see? A person more cared for, more loved, more beautiful than the most stunning flower in the garden. The inner person – you – is more esteemed than anything else in God's creation. Treasure who you are, who God created you to become. Care for yourself – your mind, heart, soul, body. You are of more importance than the most beautiful lily in the garden. Praise the Lord for he has done wondrous things.

Notice how the flowers grow...
Luke 12:27

Summer lilies grace my garden

Maplewood Gardens is filled with beautiful roses. Photographing them is such a delight. For years I have thought that the prettiest roses were those that were in bud. Tightly wrapped, they were full of potential, a bit sharp on the edges, still unknown as to what lay within. Now I find myself gravitating to the rose in full bloom. There is a softness to its petals, colors draw your attention, and you can see into its core. This particular rose reminds me of the Mercy of God. In bud form, mercy is tightly wrapped, just barely beginning to show itself. While in the open rose, mercy gently spills out from the Center. As one lives a life of mercy toward others, God, the core, is revealed. Mercy flows from and leads to God. As the fragrance of the fully opened rose fills the air, may we be both the giver of the fragrance of mercy and its recipient. A rose to you, my friend.

A Rose captured in full bloom at the Maplewood Rose Garden, Rochester, NY

A Familiar Bluet, otherwise known as a damselfly. Similar to but much smaller than a dragonfly. Doesn't God just amaze you with all these wondrous little bits of heaven? The Bluet is so very tiny, perhaps two inches at most from tip to tip. And so thin! I almost stepped on it but my attention was caught by a hint of blue where there should have only been green grass. It stayed still for so long allowing me to capture it close up. But maybe I shouldn't have been surprised to have found it. You would think I would know by now how God puts things onto our paths so we can slow down and recognize his presence. A flash of blue, a quick look, and God had my attention. I became mesmerized by this tiny creature: the thin, wispy wings, its lines no thicker than a pencil line, the big eyes which science has told me can see in all directions, and its little legs that hardly look strong enough to hold up its little body. Yet, there it is, doing its part of reminding me of the creativity of the Father. What caught your attention today?

The Mighty One
has done
great things for me;
and Holy is His name.

Luke 1:49

Damselfly resting in the grassy yard at Conseus Lake, NY

..A thorn in the flesh was given to me.

2 Corinthians 12:7

"Oh, it's a thistle!" he said sharply. As fall approaches, the once flexible, green thistle becomes dried out, brittle, and sharp. Not the favorite flower in the bunch. It seems every edge has been honed to its sharpest point and its barbs piercing. It's a weed we can live with but find annoying. We all have "thistles" in our lives. The little annoyances that aren't earthshaking but still interrupt the flow of life as we would have it. They are part of life. It is how we handle them that makes the difference. Are they just little pricks or do they become monumental stabs? Do we just say "ouch" and go on? Or do we let them fester and become disproportionally annoying? Remember, God created the thistles and they are important to creation. And He lets "thistles" be a part of our lives. They are important to our development as caring, patient, loving human beings.

Along the roadside in Upstate New York

Napa Valley, CA, is home to a multitude of vineyards, each producing its own trademark wine. This scene of such beauty is repeated over and over in all parts of the world. Awesome views remind us that we are a part of this wonderful work of God's creation. Pope Francis in Laudato Si! says: *"Nature cannot be regarded as something separate from ourselves or as a mere setting in which we live. We are part of nature, included in it and thus in constant interaction with it."* More than just being invited to be stewards of earth, it is imperative that we fulfill our role as stewards. We are dependent on the natural world around us. The natural world around us is dependent on us. One exists within the other. What is it you can do right now, right where you are, to protect nature of which you are a part?

I shall walk before the Lord in the land of the living.

Ps. 116:9

Overlooking Napa Valley, Californis

Now the one who supplies seed to the sower and bread for food will supply and multiply your seed for sowing and increase the harvest of your righteousness.

2 Corinthians 9:10

Mid-summer and the fields are ripe for harvest. The heads of wheat are ready to be gathered. It is amazing how just a few seeds can prosper into such a multitudinous supply of food. God not only provides the seeds but gives it increase. So too, God plants the seeds of love in our hearts and gives us what we need to let it bear fruit in our lives. Again, what's in your garden?

Wheat ready for harvest in a country field, Farmington, NY

May the Glory of the Lord endure forever
May the Lord be glad in these works. Ps. 104:31

"Oh, a butterfly! A monarch!" Our spirits lift when we see a butterfly flutter by. There is something about this delicate little creature that causes a sense of wonder in us. When we approach the shorter days and cooler nights, the monarchs prepare for their long migration to central Mexico. They astound us, these little bits of joy. Their winter hibernation will produce new off-spring who will fly their way back north, stopping along the way to create a new generation of monarchs, Eventually they will return to the place their ancestor would have called home. And we will be able once again to exclaim: "Oh, a butterfly! A monarch!" Doesn't God just amaze you with all these wondrous little bits of heaven?

Butterfly in a hidden garden in Salem, MA

A voice says,
"'Cry out!"
I answer,
"What shall I cry out?"
"All humankind is
grass, and all their
glory like the flower of
the field."

Isaiah 40:6

Delphinium and snapdragons create a peaceful garden. Colors blend together to form a tapestry of pinks, blues, and whites against a background of green. Nature's colors. Nature's summer gift to us. What a peaceful garden we would create if we allowed the various colors of humankind to blend together in the garden of life. And the glory of the Lord will be shown to all and they will say "Here is your God!"

Garden at Nathanial Hawthorn's house in Salem, MA

Your adornment should not be an external one ... but rather, the hidden character of the heart, expressed in the imperishable beauty of a gentle and kind dispostion which is precious in the sight of God.   1 Peter 3:3-4

I never saw the bug until I downloaded the picture into my computer. I have named this photo "God's tickling feet." The flower strikes me as a regal flower, one that is beautiful and knows that it is! It is perfect in so many ways and a bit snobby about it. And then a bug walks across it, its tickling feet breaking the mood of royalty with its bit of earthiness. And so it is with us. Whenever we begin to get puffed up over an achievement or start to develop an attitude of superiority, God sends "little tickling feet" to bring us back to earth. Humility is also a gift from God and it comes in many forms. Even as little beetles.

Flower gardens, Butterfly World, Niagara Falls, CA

Judge not.

Matthew 7:1

Look closely. What do you see? Is it the head of an owl? Or a … what? If you step back and look at the photo, you can see the owl. But it is only part of an owl. Perhaps it would be helpful to know that this was taken at Butterfly World in Ft. Lauderdale. The "owl" is actually two blue morpho butterflies with their wings overlapping as they drink the fruit nectars. The brown drab colors camouflage the translucent blues on the inside of their wings. Opened up, the blue shows up. Indeed, all is not as it seems. How easy it is to jump to conclusions based on just a few observations. How quickly we judge when we don't know all the facts. The person we consider rude may have just been given bad news; or we base a supposition on facts from a previous experience which no longer apply; or we misinterpret the actions of another. In these days of "fake news," we need to be sure of the facts before declaring something to be true. Like the blue morpho's wings, there are two sides to everything. And that can literally "color" the conclusion.

Morpho butterflies in Butterfly World, Ft. Lauderdale, FL

The lens of a camera is a marvelous piece of equipment. A zoom lens is able to bring a distant object closer or block out unwanted objects that intrude into the picture. I personally like to use the zoom lens for "up close and personal" views of things. This photo of a zinnia was taken this way. It was one of several blooms in the garden. The zoom allowed me to see details I would not have been able to see if I had included the whole garden. I would have missed the crown of tiny yellow flowers, and the dusting of pollen on the petals that tell me a bee has been at work there. The closer I got to the flower, the more blurred out the background became. I was able to cut out the distractions around the zinnia and able to focus (pun intended) on the flower itself. Our human eye doesn't see as the zoom lens does. But we can train it to look at the details. Take an object and look at it as if through a camera lens. What miracles do you see? Look at the details. What have you never noticed before? Then praise God for the wonder of it all!

*Come
and see
the works of
God...*

Ps. 66:5

Zinnia in my nieghbor's garden

*Even should
she forget,
I will never
forget you.*

Isaiah 49:15

This is one of God's beauties along a wall in Cashal, Ireland. It makes me think of my father who, in his wonderful Irish tenor voice, would sing "My Wild Irish Rose." The memory of him singing this is a treasure that I keep in the memory box of my heart. It is funny how some things can trigger a remembrance of someone we love. For a moment it brings the person alive in our hearts and causes us to smile, maybe even laugh. Or shed a silent tear. Memories are treasures with which we have been gifted. They are blessings that we humans can enjoy and they help to shape our future. Consider, too, the fact that while human minds are finite, we have a God who does not forget us, who holds us each in the palm of his hand.

"My Wild Irish Rise" grows along a wall in Cashal, Co. Tipperary, Ireland

You'll need your imagination for this one. In southern Colorado rock formations like this are around every bend. The strata of colors of this particular rock remind me of a big bowl of pasta. One can almost imagine the Creator swirling a giant fork to twist the molten rock into such formations, with a little bit of red thrown in as pasta sauce. Granted, my imagination sometimes runs wild but mostly in a humorous way. As children, it was easy to use our imaginations. We created games, plays, stories. We even found animals floating about as clouds above us. But once we "grew up" we seem to have lost our ability to imagine. Looking about us with the eyes of our imaginations allows us to be creative, to think outside the box. All kinds of possibilities exist if we open up our minds to the different, the unexpected, the surprises around us. Imagination is the color in our black and white world. What has been your color today? The fun is in seeing what we can imagine next! Ask yourself "What if…!"

Come and see
the works of
God, awesome in
the deeds done
for us.
Ps 66:5

One of the unusual red rock formations found in southern Colordo/Utah

A room with a view! Unless you are in a room that has a 360-degree window, your view is somewhat defined by the perimeters of the window frame. All is not visible at the same time. You may be able to watch the sunrise, but not the sunset. The Kodak Office building out this window, but not out of that one. The red maple out that one but not this one. We just can't see it all at once. Unless blessed with eyes on the back of our heads, we can only see what is before us. So it is with our understanding of God. There are so many facets to our God but we can see only one at a time. There is always another facet right behind us or next to us. I may see God as Creator, you may see him as loving Father, or, your experience of God is merciful and forgiving while mine may be of God as a stern task master. Sometimes we are closed in by the perimeters of that window frame, our personal experiences. Don't let that be your only view of God. Throw open the window, pull out the screen and stick your head out to get a better view. Ask God to help you acquire a "room with a view" that extends beyond the window frame.

Eye has not seen, and ear has not heard and what has not entered the human heart, what God has pre- pared for those who love him.

1 Corinthians 2:9

Window view of Holy Sepulchre Cemetery from inside Christ our Light Mausoleum, Rocheser, NY

There is something so peaceful about seeing reflections in a body of water. The sun just bounces off the trees and recreates the colors in the pond. The breeze across the open waters causes a ripple effect in the reflection making the waters look like liquid gold. The blue skies add to the crispness of the fall day and provide a contrast to the oranges and yellows. What paintbrush can duplicate these trees? Reflections can be imperfect. They might be muddied by the moving waters, or blurry because of the way the wind blows. We are reflections of the God-life within us when we bring the love of God to those around us. Like the reflections in the rippling waters, we may not always be perfect, but we do our best. And we are able to do this because Jesus showed us the human face of God. What a privilege for us to be considered reflections of God's love and mercy.

I am confident of this, that the one who began a good work in you will continue to complete it until the day of Christ Jesus.
Philippians 1:6

Fall reflected in the waters of a Durand Easmtan Park pond along Lake Ontario

He who sows sparingly will also reap sparingly, and he who sows bountifully will also reap bountifully.

2 Corinthians 9:6

The milkweed pod has popped, scattering its seed laden parachutes into the winds. You can see them floating on the breezes, hundreds of them from one pod. It is the parable of the seed: some on hard ground and never finding root, some choked out by other weeds, and some on fertile ground where next spring a new milkweed plant will sprout up. And that milkweed will, in turn, provide a shelter for the monarch butterfly larvae. Then it will be its turn to send new seeds into the wind. So it is with the seeds of kindness that we sow. Like the milkweed pod, the seeds of a kind deed may land anywhere. It may land on hard soil and be ignored, it might be rejected. But many will find a receptive soil, take root, and be a source more seeds of kindness. The miracle of one seed is that it can give life to many more. While we may not wish to be overtaken by milkweeds, wouldn't it be wonderful to be overcome by acts of kindness? Do your part today by sending out some seeds of kindness.

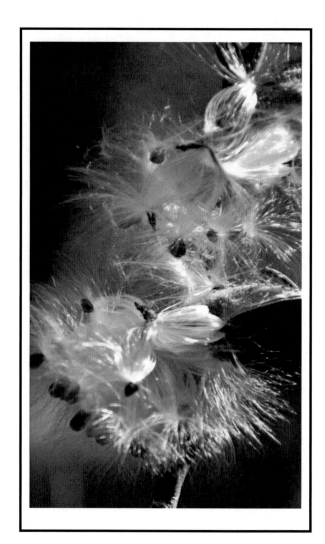

Milkweed pods are everywhere!

A view with a view! I am standing inside a covered bridge. Built in 1832, over the Ammonoosuc River, NH, it is one of the oldest surviving covered bridges. Walking across the bridge gives a great view of the river but one is quite aware of walking over the rushing waters below. Why a covered bridge? One would speculate that the biggest reason was to protect the wooden structure from the bad weather. Covers protected pedestrians and perhaps helped to keep the horses from shying away from water while crossing. Ironically, I felt safer walking across than driving across. The covered bridge is like the Lord who protects us from dangers. We may never know all the ways the Lord protects us from harm, either physical or spiritual. Sometimes we might feel the Lord has let us down when something serious happens to us. But we might never know what other harm we may have come to or know what good will come as a result. So many scripture images speak of God's protection: "Good Shepherd" John 10:11, "Strength, a fortress, a refuge, a stronghold in time of distress." Jer 16:19 "Turn to me and be safe." Is 45:22

My safety and glory are with God, my strong rock and refuge.

Ps 62:8

Swiftwater Bridge over the Ammonoosuc River, Bath, NH

An overnight dusting of new snow enhances the peace and tranquility of a Durand Eastman Pond. A moment of silent wonder as we see the beauty of God spelled out for us in nature's glory. The stillness of the crisp cold air grabs hold of our spirit and, for the moment, peace fills our heart. Take time to let its beauty sink into your being. Let its memory stay with you through the day, its peace permeating the tasks of the day. We need moments of peace like this as we encounter the high-powered challenges of the present times. Remembering moments of peace counterbalances our hectic pace. Look for the moments of peace that surround you. They are there waiting to be recognized: the giggle of a baby, the quiet of a Christmas decorated church, a conversation with a loved one, the glimpses nature provides of its beauty, the completion of a task, a moment of stillness. They are there if we have the eyes to see and a heart that is open to enjoying the moment. Peace be with you.

.....liv in peace,
and
the God of
love and peace
will be with
you."

2 Corinthians 13:11

Durand Eastman Pond on the shores of Lake Ontario, Rochester, NY

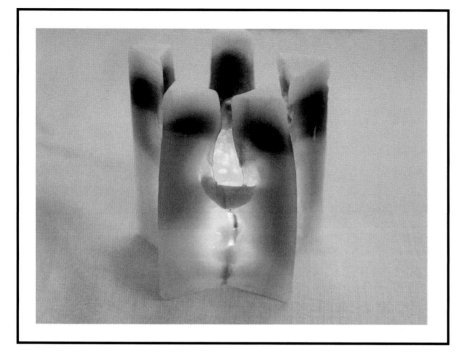

*The people
that walked in
darkness have
seen a great light...
on them the light
will shine.*

Isaiah 9:2

It started out as a gently hued candle, star shaped with 5 points. As the wick burned down through the middle, its glow spread through the wax. When the wax was spent, what remained were pillars formed from the five points. With a bit of imagination, helped along with the coloration of the wax, it is possible to see now, not a candle, but a circle of people, people through whom light shines. We are that people through whom the Light shines. Our world seems to be a dark place right now. Wars, drugs, hate crimes, distrust of one another, poverty, to say nothing of natural disasters and climate change. Where does one begin to "lighten" up our world? It begins with each one of us. The Light that is God shines through us, through our kindnesses, generosity, peace-making, comfort, forgiveness, respect for one another, love. Go back to the candle, see how the light intensifies when we stand together. We all stand together to bring Light to this world that so desperately needs it. "This little light of mine, I'm gonna let it shine." Where will your light shine these days? Whose light will shine on you?

Candle created in the "Candle With Care Studio", Mercy Center, Rochester, NY

In order to see a rainbow, certain conditions need to be present. Of course you need water drops and sunlight. The sun needs to be at a 42 degree angle behind you in order for you to see the light going through the water. Any spray of water will do as long as the sun comes at that angle. Hence this rainbow in the mists of the Middle Falls at Letchworth Park. Rainbows are special. We recognize them as a promise from God that he will be with us. How do we "see" God's presence with us? By cultivating conditions that will open us up to recognize God-with-us. Our hearts need to be readied to see what God has done in us and through us. God will never force himself on us. Daily conversations with God dispose our hearts and minds to think Gospel values. We try to live a life that is kind, compassionate and merciful. Perhaps a way to realize God-with-us is to spend some time at the end of the day reflecting on how God has been present during this day. When this begins to become a habit, we more easily recognize how God has been sending us "rainbows" all the time. And we in turn become "rainbows" as others see God reflected in us.

Draw near to
God
and he will draw
near to you."

James 4:8

Middle Falls, Genesee River, Letchworth State Park, Wyoming/Livingston Co., NY

Doesn't this picture make you want to go and get an apple to eat? They say, "An apple a day keeps the doctor away." And so it may be. This crate of freshly picked apples is filled with vitamins, fiber and all sorts of things good for us. Can't you just taste the goodness within the bright red covering. Adam and Eve and the apple in the garden aside, what a wonderful gift God has given us in the lowly apple. It can be eaten in so many amazing delectable ways: covered with a crunchy sugar coating on a candy apple, sliced and dipped in caramel, apple betty, apple sauce, pie, of course, or just held in your hand with the juices dripping down. It can be cooked with meats, made into a salad, and a thousand more ways to savor it. Our thanks to the apple growers and the growers of all kinds of foods that help "keep the doctor away." Their labors have given us a wonderful food. We need to thank God for their work, especially those migrants who move from place to place helping to provide food for our tables. They have the hardest of tasks. Go enjoy an apple! The brussels sprout doesn't have a chance.

Roadside stand, Ridge Rd., Wayne Co., NY

This delightful little garden was originally a trolley car bridge built in 1908 over the Deerfield River connecting the towns of Shelburne Falls and Buckland, MA. The increasing use of automobiles caused the trolley car business to fail and by 1927, it became a weedy, unattractive footbridge. In 1929, several women petitioned to make the old trolley bed into a garden and the "Bridge of Flowers" was created. Volunteers have been planting flowers and caring for the garden ever since. Kudos to the ladies who developed the idea, and to the many volunteers over the years. This is recycling at its finest. Not only did they rid the area of an eyesore, they beautified the entire neighborhood and made it a place that extends enjoyment to all. Praise the Lord for all the gardeners who in small and large ways improve yards and gardens throughout our cities and towns. We all benefit as we delight in the work of God's creation. We may not have bridges to recycle but perhaps we might be able to reuse a great deal of what we toss out. Recycle. It may not seem that we are accomplishing much but all of us together – what a great work we can do!

May God give to you of the dew of the heavens And of the fertility of the earth abundance of grain and wine.
Genesis 27:28

Flowering Bridge, Shelburne Falls, MA

Here is a side view of George on Mt. Rushmore in the Black Hills of South Dakota. While the profile view of the 60 foot stone sculpture is imposing, what is even more wondrous to me are the pine trees that seem to grow right out of the granite rock. There is no apparent soil for the roots to take in nourishment. There seems to be nothing the roots can hang on to. But there they are, growing taller in the passing seasons in spite of being buffeted by winds, rains and snow. My God is a rock, a stronghold, a fortress to me. He holds tight to me during the hard times of life: my struggles, my hurts. My God stands firm even when I want to move away and he is my refuge in times of need. Like the pines, I cling to my Lord and my God knowing that I will find nourishment and strength. My hope is in my God.

The Lord is my life's refuge;
of whom am I afraid?

Ps. 27:2

Mt. Rushmore in the Black Hills of South Dakota

*The Lord
will guide you
always.*

Isiah 58:11

The staircase spirals upward to the top of the lighthouse. Its narrow steps are fastened securely to the center pole, the outside wall serving as an aid to balance your ascent/descent. It's not an easy climb, especially if you have big feet. But it is that center pole that gives the backbone to the lighthouse. It holds the weight of the steps and keeps them in balance. It allows the steps to seem almost suspended in space. Without the center there would be no spiral staircase. Reflect on the center of your life. Is God at the Center? Do you cling to this Center to give you the balance you need to lead a good faith-filled life? If we break away from the Center we lose the support we need to keep our lives secure. Remember how unbalanced you feel when God is not at your Center, when other things and possessions take the place as the "most important" in your life. If we are mindful of being God-centered, then we are assured that God will keep us safe and on the right step.

The Charlotte/Genesee Lighthouse, commissioned in 1822. Lake Ave., Charlotte, NY

On a fall walk through the neighborhood I came across this wandering pumpkin vine. It somehow lost its GPS signal and worked its way into a neighbor's lilac bush. Tightly wedged in, it took serious consideration on how to extricate it from its unusual perch without causing any damage. When we depend too heavily on the GPS in our cars we sometimes end up in unexpected places, often not at all where we wanted to be. While using a "global positioning system" is a good thing for people with no sense of direction or in a new environment, we have an even better GPS: it is called "God's Positioning Service." It's free and its directions are easy to follow. Its manual can be found in an understandable language in the Bible. When we make a wrong turn, this GPS helps us to "recalculate" and get back on track. Then we are positioned to bring compassion and mercy to those we meet on the way. Is your GPS in sync with God's?

I am the Way,
the Truth
and the Life.

John 14:6

Misdirected pumpkin on Whittington Rd., Irondequoit, NY

*From the
rising of the sun
to its setting let
the name of the
Lord
be praised.*

Psalm 113:3

Earlier in the summer I had witnessed the rising of the sun on the Atlantic coast. And here I am seeing the setting sun on the Pacific Coast. But not on the same day! There is a lot of country in between the two oceans. Likewise there is a lot of time between the rising and the setting of the sun. The Psalmist tells us that during that time span we should be praising the Lord. Does that mean that I must constantly be thinking of the Lord and be verbally praising him the whole day? That is rather an impossibility. Not even the most saintly among us is able to do that. What is asked of us is that our thoughts, words and deeds of the day be offered up to the Lord as acts of praise. If we are mindful of the fact that we are created in the image and likeness of God, then our actions will be God-like. This means that we are giving praise to God for all he has given to us. When we are merciful, compassionate, loving, and kind to others, then we are showing the human face of God to others. Showing God to others is giving praise to the Lord, "from the rising of the sun to its setting."

Pacific Ocean Sunset from the shores of Santa Cruz, CA

Each year the Orchid Society of Rochester holds a show at the Eisenhart Auditorium. Each orchid is unique in size, shape and color. They look so fragile on such thin stems but are quite hardy. However, some need more care than others. Your prom orchids they are not! But each adds its unique beauty to the world around us. One could liken this vast array of beauty to our human race. We each add beauty to our own spot on the globe. We are a vast assortment of people. Not only in race, but in personality, thoughts, feelings. Some of us may need a bit more assistance or care than others. But we are a hardy bunch. We are able to rebound from difficulties, hurts, fears. We have hope. And together we make a wonderful display of talents and gifts. Everyone of us is a part of this show. In spite of any differences among us we are, all of us, a gift from God. We are a gift to each other, we are a sign of hope for the future.

*Before I
formed you in
the womb I knew
you.*

Jeremiah 1:5

Annual Orchid Show, Rochester, NY

*You made the moon
to mark the seasons;
The sun knows the
hour of its setting."*

Psalm 104:19

Until we landed people on the moon, the moon has always been mysterious. No, it is not made of cheese. And there is no "man in the moon." The brighter color of the rising moon is due to the light having to travel through the atmosphere to get to us. Pictures taken by satellite reveal the nature of the surface of the moon. The more we understand what it is, the less mysterious the moon has become. Isn't that true of our relationships with others. The more we know about people, learn about them, the better we understand them and they are not so mysterious. We find that we are all basically the same. We have the same emotions, personalities, and intelligences. The differences are really on the surface. We often fear what we don't know or understand. Can you make it your goal to learn about people of other cultures. You might begin with trying to understand the reason that there is a caravan of people at our southern door.

Summer moonrise through the pines of Canandaigua Lake's shore.

For I know well the plans in mind for you," declares the Lord, "plans to prosper you and not to harm you, plans to give you hope and a future.

Jeremiah 29:11

Let go? What do you mean, "Let go," Lord? Well, I am rather attached to this tree branch. Oh, you mean that is the problem? But I like hanging around here. This tree gave life to me, and look, I have changed already – I mean, I was once green and now I am a golden leaf. But Lord, what will happen to me if I let go? If I let you direct my life? I am afraid, Lord. What do you mean that when I fall to the ground I will change? Into what? Oh, you're saying it will be into something even better, that because of me and the nutrients in me, new life will grow, that I will enable a new leaf to take my place giving shade to those who rest under the tree. Will it hurt, Lord? Ah, you will be there to make it easier. You know I like to hang onto the known and secure. Still, if I let go and let you direct me, I will find my place, my purpose in this world. And when I get too comfortable there, you will invite me to let go again. I am your creation, Lord. My ultimate purpose is to give you praise and glory. So, one more strong gust of wind, Lord, and here I go! Whee! what a ride down! Now do with me what you will.

Leaves, leaves, everywhere there are leaves!

*"What do you want
Me to do for you?"
They answered,
"Lord,
let our eyes
be opened."*

Matthew 20:32-34

This snowy owl resides at the Seneca Park Zoo. Because of previous injuries, she is not able to fly away. The female owl has brownish black spots on its feathers. The adult male is all white. One of the amazing things about an owl is its ability to turn its neck 270 degrees. It gives it a scope of vision that gives new meaning to a teacher's "eyes on the back of her head" belief. The gift of sight is something we so take for granted. When we are fitted with our first pair of glasses, we start to realize how precious it is. Sometimes we need to have cataracts removed as our vision gets cloudy. But vision isn't limited to what we look at, it is also a way to describe a hope for the future, an idea, a plan to attain something new. Seeing is also understanding: "I see what you are saying." It doesn't mean that words are floating in front of us, but that we grasp what the person means. Sometimes this vision gets cataracts, too. Its original vision is cloudy, muddied. We no longer clearly "see" what another person means. Then we need to do whatever is necessary to clear it up. We need "new lenses" to refocus our hopes and dreams, to open our eyes to what is possible, to see each other more clearly. "We want our sight."

Snowy Owl at Seneca Park Zoo, Rochester, NY

Do you believe? This might be the question when 7, 8, and 9 year olds begin to doubt their belief in Santa. To discover that Santa doesn't really exist as a jolly old soul can be shattering for some, for others a matter of fact moving on. So, too, they question the Tooth Fairy, the Easter Bunny, the Great Pumpkin. How, then, do we help these new "non-believers" transition into children who believe in an invisible God. We start with the story of Jesus, who became visible to us all. We talk about his life, his miracles, his presence with us each day. Children copy what they see adults do. If we praise God, thank God, ask for his help in times of need in the presence of children, they will see that we have a belief in God, in Jesus. If we take time to worship God in our houses of prayer, this, too, will show the importance of believing in God. Sure, there are always the teen-age years, but if a child is raised in a house of faith, they will find their way back. Provide them with opportunities to develop their own relationship with God. Encourage them to "Believe."

nd they said to the woman, "We no longer believe because of your word; for we have heard for ourselves..."

John 4:42

Ornament found in a Christmas display

The Lord is my light and my salvation
whom do I fear?
Wait for the Lord, take courage, be stouthearted.
Wait for the Lord. Ps. 27:1,14

This little scrub tree clings perilously on the edge of Bryce Canyon, Utah. It appears that the slightest wind would blow it off its perch. But it is hanging in there! Its roots cling to the stronghold deep beneath the surface. Taking its sustenance and strength from the source, it will prosper and grow. It is just going to take time. After all, it is just a little tree. We have our Sustenance and Strength in the Lord. This will take us through the winds of stress, sadness, and fear. We just have to wait on the Lord, knowing that God is our stronghold. Why should we be afraid?

At the edge of Bryce Cnyon, Utah

The actual size of this dahlia was about the size of a dinner plate, its petals unfolding themselves from the center. Extra care with plenty of water and plant food enabled it to grow to such a size. It brings to mind how the Word of God dwells in us and, nourished by scripture, sacrament, and deeds, the Word expands out from our center, God, and spreads into a beautiful expression of mercy and peace. What nourishment do you need to feed the Word within you? What will empower the Word of God to use you to speak it?

Your word
is a lamp
for my feet,
A light
for my path.

Ps. 119:105

Dahlia in a friend's garden on Beach Ave., Charlotte, NY

*The Lord said to Moses: 'Strike the rock, and the water will flow
from it for the people to drink.'
This Moses did, in the presence of the elders of Israel.*

Exodus 17:6

Cool, sweet, refreshing water. How blessed we are to have such easy access to this basic human right. Let us not take it for granted. We know what we need to do to preserve the supply of fresh water. Turn off the faucets, keep pollutants out of our rivers and streams, use organic fertilizers, pour less water into a glass if you are only going to drink a bit of it. Let's do it! Blessed are those who give drink to the thirsty by their careful use of this natural resource and who provide ways for those who lack clean water to have their share of the earth's water supply.

Waterfall at Corbett's Glen, Penfield, NY

There is an appointed time for everything.

Ecclesiastes 3:1

I have titled this photo "God's Crayon Box." Fall is that time of the year when God gets out his paints and begins to color the world in new and brilliant pigments. It happens subtly, gradually at first. A leaf here, a flower there. Sometimes just part of a branch or tree. So subtle that we might find the artist has been at work and we never even noticed. Gone are the bright lemon greens of spring, the warm greens of summer. We may awaken one morning and find the world has changed to bright reds, oranges and gold. The seasons move on. So, too, with our lives. We are subtly changing; we are not who we were yesterday nor who we will be tomorrow. God has been at work in us as well as in the world around us. We may wake up one morning and realize we have changed, been changed. Sometimes it is good to reflect back on the different changes that have led us to where we are now. In doing so we will see that the Artist has always been at work in our lives, guiding us through our various seasons with wonderful colors and graces.

Leaf found along the roadside on Rt. 1A, Portsmouth, NH

So I went down to the potter's house and there he was, working at the wheel.

Jeremiah 18:3

Beginning with a shapeless lump of clay, the potter began spinning his wheel. His hands worked the magic, gently pulling the clay into the shape he desired. Too much pressure on the top would make a lopsided pot. Not a lot of pressure on the inside, that would make a too thin wall that could crack in the kiln. Gently, gently, he coaxed the clay into the image he had envisioned. If a mistake happened, then he would break down the clay and begin again. He never would give up on the piece of clay nor the potential it held within. Giving one last push on the spinning wheel, he removed the vase and set it aside for the final touches and readied it for the kiln. Soon it would be ready to fulfill the purpose for which it was created. Picture yourself as that lump of clay being gently formed into who you are meant to be. God, the potter, is not finished with us yet. We won't be finished until our life on earth is done. We are still in the process of being perfected. God doesn't give up on us when something goes wrong in our lives. He is constantly present, gently molding us, adding beautiful finishes of compassion, joy, kindness, love. Let the Potter's hands guide you.

Potter, Genesee County Museum, Caldonia/Mumford, NY

Learn to savor how good the Lord is. Ps. 34:9

It's apple pickin' time! One can almost smell the homemade apple pie, or apple betty. Such a wonderful gift from our Creator God. It is a fruit that touches all our senses (which also are a gift from God). We pick the apple, hold it in our hands to feel the smooth texture. We hear the crisp snap as we bite into it and savor the sweet/tart taste. And lastly, we smell the fruity tang of fall. Being aware of our senses brings us into contact with the natural world…as well as the Divine. Let your senses do the talking. When and how did your senses talk to you today?

Apple Farm, Victor, NY

God is able to make every grace abundant for you, so that in all things, always having all you need, you many have an abundance for every good work.

2 Corinthians 9:8

The golds of these maples take your breath away. As they fall, they create a golden carpet for us to walk upon. Reflecting on this scene, in this particular place (Holy Sepulchre Cemetery), the carpet of gold symbolizes to me a carpet of blessings bestowed on us by our loving God. We have been so blessed! We have what we need: food, shelter, friends, family. And we have so much more. Can we name our leaves of blessings? Sheltered by the golden trees, and carpeted by their leaves are our most sacred of blessings, those who rest in the ground of this holy place: family, friends, neighbors, and even the strangers, who have been the source of so many of the blessings in our lives. Is it any wonder that some of my most beautiful fall photos are taken in a cemetery? Praise God for all the blessings in our lives!

Golden maples, Holy Sepulchre Cemetery, Lake Ave., Rochester, NY

Harvest season is that wonderful time of the year when we get to enjoy the fruits of summer labor. We have been filling ourselves with the summer vegies and fruits: zucchini, berries, carrots, peaches, etc. Now, when the season turn to fall, it is the feast of grapes, apples, root vegetables, squash, pumpkins. How blessed we are! All this bounty evokes in us an "attitude of gratitude" as we praise the Creator for all the good gifts he has bestowed on us. Along with this blessing comes a responsibility. We are God's hands and stewards of all his bounty. Let us seek out ways to share that with which we have been blessed.

Give thanks
always
and for
everything
in the name of our
Lord Jsus Christ
to God
the Father.

Ephesians 5:20

Grapes on Wickham Farms, Penfield, NY waiting to be picked

As the days begin to get shorter and darker, the signal goes out for many of our birds to begin their migratory trek to southern points. Migratory birds seem to follow the same routes year after year which are called "flyways." It is thought that as the summer supply of food dwindles and the cold settles in, the birds have an inner survival sense that starts them on their way. In spring, as the north begins to warm and food begins to be plentiful again, they make the same trek back north. Their routes involve paths that have healthy nesting grounds and stop-over sites for resting and feeding. The problem facing our bird population is that many of their stopping places along migratory routes are being "civilized" and the birds face exhaustion and starvation with no place to stop. We need to work to preserve these areas for the safety of the birds and the balance of nature or we will find ourselves wondering why our summer birds are no longer singing in the branches of our gardens.

Beside them the birds of heaven nest; among the branches they sing.

Ps. 104:12

"Birds of Paradise" Bird Sanctuary (no longer open), Buffalo, NY

Give us this day our daily bread.

Matthew 6:11

We've lost our touch for making bread. It is so much easier to just go to the store to pick up a loaf for supper. Making bread is a process and all processes need time and often patience. The rising element, yeast, needs to ferment before adding it into the flour. Then there is the wait for the rising of the dough, done in a warm place with no drafts. Finally, shaped into loaves, it rises once more before being baked. There is nothing like the smell of homemade bread just out of the oven. Ah, but it is so worth the time and energy. However, we are too much in a hurry. Bread is one of the oldest prepared foods, dating back almost 30,000 years. In many cultures bread is a metaphor for that which is sustaining life. In Christianity it is one of the elements of Eucharist. Jesus names himself as the "Bread of Life." Bread is meant to be broken and shared and we do this at the meal called "Eucharist." These loaves of bread were being sold at the Public Market. But why not make some of your own. Share it with a friend, if you have any left after tasting it yourself. Mmmmm, melted butter, strawberry jam!!!!

Bread for Sale at the Rochester Public Market

The Five Arch Bridge on route 39 in the town of Avon, NY, was a viaduct that once carried the Genesee Valley railroad over Conesus Outlet. By April of 1859, the train connected the towns of Avon, Geneseo, and Mt. Morris with the city of Rochester. Sounds like the first "park and ride" concept! Initially it was a steam engine that traveled the route. By1940, other modes of transportation took over and the railroad was officially closed. The Five Arches remain as a picnic area and as a hiking trail. Retelling the stories of the past help us feel connected to the history it relates. Retelling the stories of our families keeps alive the people and events of our personal history. Given the increased use of electronics today, it might be an interesting adventure to retell electronically our history for the future generations. We have a book that tells the stories and experiences of our Judeo/Christian heritage. It is called the Bible. The Bible keeps us connected with our faith traditions and offers a guide for today's living. It is a living Word that, unlike stone structures of the past, continues our faith stories.

Remains of an old viaduct on Rt. 39, south of Avon, NY

Walking up the gorge of Stony Brook Park brings you to one of its many waterfalls. We can't help but notice the shale rock on the sides of the gorge, layer upon layer. In many ways this could be a metaphor for us. We are made up of many layers describing who we are. Some are layers that will never change: being a Mom, a Dad, a sibling, race, blood type, etc. Some are layers that will change as the waters of time go by: profession, physical characteristics (weight, height, gray hair or none at all), mental capacity, and many more changeable attributes common to our human nature, even sinfulness. But there is one part of us that will never change: that of being a "child of God." No matter how many times we turn away from God, God is still with us. Msgr. Richard Burns always addressed a person no matter how old they were, from 2 to 92, as "Child of God!" For that indeed is who we are. And the waterfall? The waters of grace that flow over us, wearing away the bits and pieces until we stand as we truly are: a "Child of God."

See what love the Father has bestowed on us that we may be called the children of God. Yet so we are.

John 3:1

Stoney Brook State Park, Dansville, NY

This little fellow was content to sit on Karen's finger while its wings dried out from the rain storm. The dragon fly rarely holds still long enough to allow even a quick photo. So this was a unique opportunity to see its intricate details. The total wingspan is twice that of its body size. The detail in the wing membranes is perfect and seems thinner than a human hair. And yet these wings allow it to effortlessly dart about the garden. Some dragon flies can fly up to 22–30 mph but cruise at about 9 mph. and can change direction midflight. No wonder the dragonfly is so hard to photograph. The eyes are enormous and can see in multiple directions. Most varieties of dragon flies live near a body of water and wetlands. They are great at the disposing of insect pests in the gardens. But with the destruction of the wetland and rainforests, many dragonflies, like other creatures, are endangered. Take some time to stop and just look at some object in nature. What lessons can be learned from it? What do we learn about God our Creator by close scrutiny of his creatures? There are marvels everyday.

Bless the Lord,
all creatures
everywhere
in God's
domain.

Ps 103:22

Dragon Fly, McKee Gardens, Vero Beach, FL

My soul,
be at rest in
God alone,
from whom
comes
my hope.

Ps. 62:6

The sun sets in the west and night begins to fall over the city. The traffic rush is over and the day begins to quiet. Most people are settling in for the evening. This is a time for renewal, for rejuvenation of the body and spirit. Stress seems to be ruling our days more and more. We feel stressed when our mental list of things to do isn't done. It puts us on edge and being on edge doesn't bode well for good family/personal relationships. And the cycle of stress continues. So we don't finish all we intended for the day. I don't think anyone of us can say we got it all done. We need to remind ourselves that the sky is NOT going to fall in if it isn't all completed. What's left to do can be done tomorrow. (Unless, of course, your first grader tells you at 8 pm that she told the teacher you would make cookies for the treat tomorrow!) Leave stress at the door when you come home. Yes, sometimes it is hard to do. Perhaps deliberately putting our cares into the hands of the Lord who has promised to lift our burdens might help us. Sometimes just naming the stress to someone else helps to relieve it. God is a good listener. Sleep well tonight!

City Skyline at sunset, Rochester, NY

For nineteen years, this seasonal display of unique and hand-crafted gingerbread houses deck the hallways and rooms of the George Eastman House. Most are made by families and groups such as schools, scouts, and businesses. Of course, the foundation is gingerbread (can't you just smell it baking!) but, enhanced by royal frosting and colorful candies, it needs to be a solid foundation to hold all the added decorations. A lop-sided foundation doesn't bode well for the finished product. The houses are later auctioned off and the proceeds used to further the projects of the George Eastman House. The importance of a good foundation is essential in a well-lived life. It is a firm base upon which we rest the enhancements of our lives. A good foundation holds us up when we are struck by the calamities, misfortunes, and challenges of daily living. It gives us good understanding. How do we establish a good foundation? There's a great book of directions available to us. In fact, you probably already have one on your bookshelf. As you are building your foundation, use the Bible as your source. You can't go wrong with it.

Everyone who listens these words of Mine and acts on them, will be like a wise man who built his house on the rock.

Matthew 7:24

Gingerbread Houses Exhibit, George Eastman House, Rochester, NY

Every year the farmer who works this land plants sunflower seeds. Thousands of them! Just so we can enjoy the beauty of creation. Not only do we enjoy the sunny blooms, so also do the bees. There have to be at least three bees for each flower. Gratefully they are too busy gathering pollen to worry about the human spectators. The birds, especially the purple finch, feast on the seeds. What a feast spread out before our eyes: Cheer for our souls, pollen for the bees, and seeds for the birds. Who can ask for a more glorious sight.

From the rising of the sun to its setting,
Let the name of the Lord be praised. Ps. 113:3

Sunflower Field, Higgins Farm, Rt. 65, Mendon, NY

God has gotten creative once again, this time using his white crayon to sketch in this peaceful winter scene in Seneca County. Or, to put it another way, because "white" is the presence of all colors in the color spectrum, God went all out and used all his crayons to create this beautiful sight. White is what the light reflected back to our eyes is when the wavelengths of all colors are absorbed. Colors that are not completely absorbed are what give the contrast to the total white picture. Simply said, all colors play a role in God's creation. We need the different wave lengths of light to see the different colors that make up our universe. Can we stretch that to say that we need all people reflecting the Light of God to make up our human race? Hopefully, we will continue to recognize that all the colors of God's crayon box are needed to reflect the beauty of his creation, that it is possible to blend all of us together, that no crayon is greater than the others in the box. May your day today be filled with a rainbow of color.

We know that all things work for good for those who love God.

Romans 8:28

Hoar Frost decorates the trees and fields in Seneca Co., NY

Come and see the works of God, awesome in the deeds done for us.

Ps. 66:5

Each year, the George Eastman House in Rochester, NY celebrates Mr. Eastman's passion for bulb flowers with a glorious display of all varieties and colors of tulips, daffodils, iris, hyacinths, and more – all grown from little bulbs. This display is usually in mid-winter, February, when we all yearn to see the promise of spring. These little bulbs, some as small as your thumb, are covered with dried up layers of tissue-thin skin that protect the inner core. To the non-gardener, one wonders how something that ugly can become something so beautiful. Yet the gardener knows that at the core lies the promise of something great. With care and nurturing, that ugly little bulb transforms into a flower of amazing complexity. So it is with people. Sometimes all we see are the dried up exteriors and turn away. Yet each person has an inner core which holds something beautiful. There is promise there to be discovered. Let us be patient gardeners to each other, caring for and nurturing the goodness in one another. Let us allow the Master Gardener to work his miracle is us and in each other. We are creations of promise and beauty.

Spring bulb floral display, George Eastman House, Rochester, NY

Credits

Made in the USA
Middletown, DE
03 November 2021